30 *plus*

TRIOS FOR FLUTE

by

John Cacavas

These trio arrangements were scored and compiled basically for recreational playing, yet keeping in mind many of the problems confronting young players.

The music is carefully phrased, and unlike many books of this nature, dynamics play an important part.

The two categories of compositions are those of a serious nature and folk or traditional songs.

Although it is recommended that a trio play this book, it will also be satisfactory for duets.

The repeats are optional, but for public performance they should be observed. The melody is always in the first part; for that reason players may alternate parts.

Contents

EL 2357

Russian Song

P. TSCHAIKOWSKY
(1840 - 1893)

With motion

EL 2357

Big Rock Candy Mountain

TRADITIONAL

Black is the Color of My True Love's Hair

TRADITIONAL

When the Saints Go Marching In

TRADITIONAL

Northern Song
(Saebygga)

GRIEG

Minuet

ECCLES

Bourreé

LEOPOLD MOZART

Allegretto

HAYDN

Shenandoah

TRADITIONAL

Saraband
(from Suite XI)

HANDEL

Skip to My Lou

TRADITIONAL

Aura Lee

FOLK SONG

Deep River

SPIRITUAL

The Lonesome Road

Prelude
(Op. 28 No. 7)

To A Wild Rose

EDWARD MacDOWELL

EL 2357

Greensleeves

OLD ENGLISH

Largo

CORELLI

Arietta

D. G. TURK

Joshua

SPIRITUAL

Little Brown Jug

TRADITIONAL

Chorale

ROBERT SCHUMANN

Cockles and Mussels

IRISH

Saraband

HENRY PURCELL

Bagatelle

ANTONIO DIABELLI

Sonata

DOMENICO SCARLATTI

Gavotte

Moderato

WITTHAVER

Polka Russe

GLINKA

Sweet Betsy from Pike

TRADITIONAL

Air

MOZART

Fanfare

Trumpet Piece

PURCELL